This book is on loan from
Library Services for Schools

www.cumbria.gov.uk/libraries/schoolslibserv

County Council

STREET THEATRE

R. J. Storey

EDGE
FRANKLIN WATTS

LONDON·SYDNEY

To watch some great street theatre videos, scan the QR codes with your smartphone. See pages 5, 6, 8, 10 and 15.

First published in 2013 by
Franklin Watts
338 Euston Road
London NW1 3BH

Franklin Watts Australia
Level 17/207 Kent Street
Sydney NSW 2000

Series editor: Adrian Cole

Packaged for Franklin Watts by Storeybooks
rita@storeybooks.co.uk
Designer: Rita Storey

A CIP catalogue record for this book is available
from the British Library.

Printed in China

Dewey classification: 792'.002

ISBN
(HB): 978 1 4451 1945 8
(Library ebook): 978 1 4451 2585 5

Franklin Watts is a division of Hachette Children's Books,
an Hachette UK company
www.hachette.co.uk

Photo acknowledgements
aodaodaodaod/Shutterstock.com: 6. Artizani: 5. Bikeworldtravel/Shutterstock.com: 22. BrokenSphere/ Wikimedia Commons: 10. Diaframma/Shutterstock.com: 9. Foto011/Shutterstock.com: 19. Francine Daveta/Retna Ltd./Corbis: 7. i-stock: 3. jan kranendonk/Shutterstock.com: 12. Kavun Kseniia/Shutterstock.com: 11. Kobby Dagan/Shutterstock.com: 4. MARKA/Alamy: 8 – 9. meunierd/Shutterstock.com: 20. Peter Stroh/Alamy: 15.Radoslaw Lecyk/Shutterstock.com: 16. Ruthven Carstairs/Alamy: 14. spirit of america/Shutterstock.com: 18 – 19. Stephen Finn/Shutterstock.com:1, 13. Shutterstock: 3, 5, 17, 21.

Every attempt has been made to clear copyright. Should there be any inadvertent omission, please apply to the Publishers for rectification.

Contents

Street Theatre

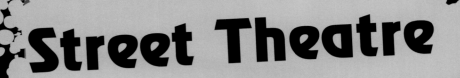

Street theatre is free entertainment in a public place.

Performers choose places where they can be seen by a lot of people.

Street performers include fire-eaters, jugglers, musicians . . .

"We take great theatre onto the streets."

. . . actors, dancers, comedians and mime artists . . .

. . . or even a giant, red inflatable lobster.

Buskers

Buskers are mainly musicians. They play music on the streets.

If people like what they hear, they give them money.

For some musicians, busking can lead to a recording contract.

Anita Maj
Anita was discovered busking on the London Underground.

Circus Acts

Circus acts are some of the most thrilling street performances.

Covent Garden in London is a popular place to watch circus acts.

Jugglers, acrobats, stilt walkers, tightrope walkers and fire-eaters often attract large crowds of people.

Sardine Family Circus

Sardine Family Circus is a family of young circus performers.

They perform on the streets of San Francisco while also attending circus school.

Living Statues

A living statue is a mime artist who sits or stands very still, pretending to be a statue.

Mime artists use clever costumes and make-up to make themselves look like stone or metal.

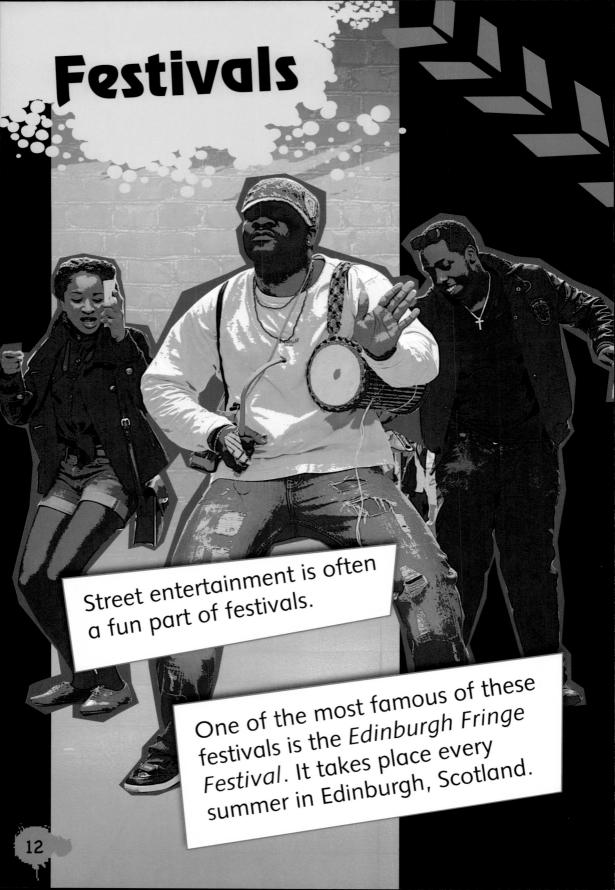

Festivals

Street entertainment is often a fun part of festivals.

One of the most famous of these festivals is the *Edinburgh Fringe Festival*. It takes place every summer in Edinburgh, Scotland.

"Street theatre can be crazy!"

At the *Edinburgh Fringe Festival*, performers come out onto the streets to persuade people to come and watch their shows.

Giant Puppets

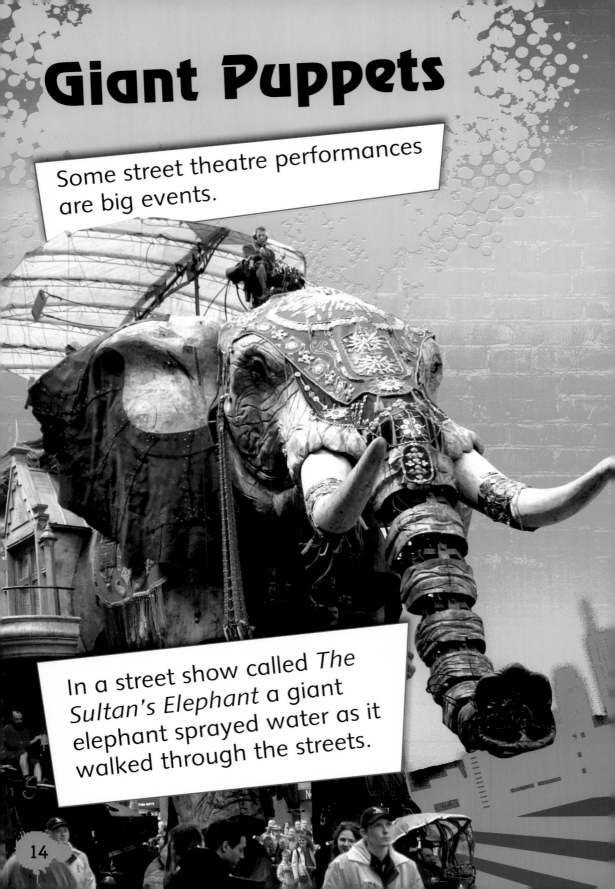

Some street theatre performances are big events.

In a street show called *The Sultan's Elephant* a giant elephant sprayed water as it walked through the streets.

In Berlin, a massive deep-sea diver puppet and a little giantess puppet took part in an open-air performance around the city.

Chinese New Year

At Chinese New Year, Chinese people all over the world celebrate with family and friends.

People make long, colourful dragons. They dance the dragons along the streets in noisy parades.

"A dragon dance is exciting to watch."

In San Francisco, it takes a team of more than 100 men and women to carry the dragon.

Parades

All over the world, parades are a way of celebrating important dates or events.

Parades march down the streets of a town or city. People watch and cheer as the parade passes by.

In a parade there are often marching bands, majorettes and dancers on decorated floats.

19

Carnival

Carnivals are colourful, noisy street parties.

'It's party time!'

Notting Hill in London, Rio de Janeiro in Brazil and Venice in Italy are all famous for their carnivals.

In Venice, many people wear masks at carnival time.

People dress up in costumes and parade alongside decorated floats. The crowds dance to the music and have fun.

Samba bands often play at carnivals.

Glossary

Acrobat An entertainer who performs gymnastic moves as part of his or her act.

Busker An entertainer who performs in a public place in the hope of being given money.

Carnival A large public celebration.

Chinese New Year A Chinese spring festival celebrated by Chinese people all over the world.

Circus act An entertainment that uses circus skills such as juggling, acrobatics, tightrope or stilt walking or fire-eating.

Dragon dance A Chinese dance traditionally performed at Chinese new year celebrations.

Edinburgh Fringe Festival An international arts festival held every August in Edinburgh, Scotland.

Festival An organised programme of events such as comedy or theatre.

Fire-eater A performer who entertains an audience by pretending to swallow fire.

Float The flat platform behind a tractor or truck. People in costume stand or dance on decorated floats to take part in a parade.

Living statue A street entertainer who pretents to be a statue.

Majorettes Girls who twirl a baton and march with a band.

Mime artists Performers who act out a story without speaking.

Parade A public procession to celebrate an important date or event.

Puppet A jointed model with a mechanism for making it move.

Samba A type of music and dance which originated in Brazil.

To watch some great street theatre in action, scan the QR codes on these pages or copy the links below into your browser.

5 http://www.youtube.com/watch?v=Obnh0dqvSds&feature=player_embedded

6 http://www.youtube.com/watch?v=8CHohYnptFM

8 http://www.youtube.com/watch?v=TRxBEQVzic0

10 http://www.youtube.com/watch?NR=1&feature=endscreen&v=shFZZkLEjOY

15 http://www.youtube.com/watch?v=8PHfmljjsZE

Index

Websites

www.artizani.net/
From the company that taught Ant and Dec to walk a tightrope take a tour through how a street theatre company works and the sort of shows they perform. The site has video clips of lots of crazy shows and walkabout acts.

www.royal-de-luxe.com/en/pictures-wall/
Find out more about the Royal de Luxe street theatre company including backstage video footage.

www.bbc.co.uk/blast/183858
Top tips on how to perform physical street theatre.

Please note: every effort has been made by the Publishers to ensure that the websites in this book contain no inappropriate or offensive material. However, because of the nature of the Internet, it is impossible to guarantee that the contents of these sites will not be altered. We strongly advise that Internet access is supervised by a responsible adult.